Whistling Through

Jeffrey Betcher

Whistling Through

978-1-7373075-4-9 (Paperback)
978-1-7373075-5-6 (Ebook)

Cover design by Amit Dey
Book design by Amit Dey

Table of Contents

Preface

Poet, fiction writer, and community activist Jeffrey Lee Betcher was born on June 6, 1960 in Mount Vernon, Ohio. He moved to San Francisco in the 1980s, taking a job as program and operations director for the Family Violence Prevention Fund. In his Bayview neighborhood Jeffrey was co-founder and then leader of Quesada Gardens Initiative, which nurtured a dangerous neighborhood into a warm, flourishing community by organizing neighbors to grow a flower and vegetable garden on a trash-strewn median strip. Through all this, Jeffrey kept writing. In addition to *Whistling Through*, his literary works include *The Fucking Seasons: Selected Poems 1986 to 2016* and a number of short stories about living as a gay man in 1980s San Francisco.

My own friendship with, and mentorship of, Jeffrey Betcher was born and fulfilled within a beautiful, otherworldly one-year framework. I had the joy of meeting Jeffrey on October 30, 2016, the day before my 60th birthday. I had traveled from Maine to San Francisco as a fellow of a progressive think tank called the Black Earth Institute, to attend a major witchy event of the year in the United States: the Spiral Dance. Pioneered by Starhawk in 1979, danced by hundreds in the Kezar Pavilion in Golden Gate Park, this impressive ritual celebrates the season of Halloween/

Samhain— a magical time to honor and connect with those who have transitioned to the next world.

I had long wanted to attend Spiral Dance and this year was the perfect moment. The poet, scholar, and force of witch-nature Patricia Monaghan, whom I had met when she invited me to accept a fellowship to Back Earth Institute and who had grown into a beloved friend, mentor, and supporter, had passed over in 2012. Her loss was still felt as a painful abyss in my life, as well as in the life of her husband Michael McDermott and of many who knew her. The Spiral Dance ritual, held amid dozens of intricate, eloquent, elaborate altars to the dead, was the ideal opportunity to pay fitting tribute to Patricia's spirit and the power of our memories of her.

I landed and went straight to Golden Gate Park. I would be staying at the Bayview house of one of Patricia's numerous friends, but I didn't have time to drop off my bag there; I had to meet Michael at the Pavilion to build our altar for Patricia. In the bright, open entry, I was stopped in my tracks by a huge mandala on the floor—an exquisite, fragrant wheel in an elaborate design created from thousands of painstakingly arranged red, orange, yellow, blue, white, and purple flower petals. Reverently, we entered the cavernous hall and found the spot to set up our altar to Patricia, full of scarves, candles, goddess statues, copies of her many books, and photos of her delightful, laughing face. We lit the candles and then moved slowly around the edges of the room contemplating the altars to the various beloved dead, not only friends and family members but also abortions and miscarriages, victims of injustice, wise women murdered in the witch-burnings, species driven to extinction, and the pain of mother Earth.

Then came the performance, the dancers in bright scarves and gowns enacting the elements, and finally the Spiral Dance itself where hundreds of us held hands and swayed and curved until the whole room writhed and spiraled chanting in the darkness, carrying ourselves and each other into a single shared awareness of temporality, exquisite mortality. We created a magical space in which death and life connected, sang, and danced together. And it was time to go.

It was a little tricky for the cab driver to find the house in Bayview. As it happened my son Julian was visiting San Francisco that same weekend, and the host I had not yet met had generously offered to put him up as well. The two of us peered out the cab windows now, at what seemed to be a tangle of sunflowers and tomatoes in the darkness, trying to make sense of it all. I had been given only the name Jeffrey Betcher and an address in the Quesada Gardens neighborhood. I hadn't realized Quesada Gardens was not a neighborhood but a single street —or that the street had a big garden in the middle of it. The tall plants, still thriving in the California fall, made it necessary to drive all the way to the end of the block, unclear what was on the other side of the street, then turn around and drive slowly up the other side to find the house number.

But as soon as we found the address, it seemed as if we had always known it. The house was a beautifully painted and restored Victorian, bright and open. Jeffrey was one of the warmest, most welcoming hosts I had ever encountered. He laughed and joked and gave us a tour of the house and saw to our every comfort. After Julian went to sleep, Jeffrey and I stayed up late into the night drinking tea and comparing notes on our lives. He told me how dangerous and decayed the area had been when he moved into the house in the 1990s, how much persistence the Quesada Gardens Initiative had taken, and how satisfying it had been when his neighbors came together to plant the magnificent garden on the median (the next morning, I would see Jeffrey's magnetic powers in action as a variety of neighbors dropped in one by one, clearly fully at home in his home, to borrow things and update him on neighborhood news). We talked about Patricia Monaghan, witchiness, art, and spirituality as well, and I learned that Jeffrey was also a creative writer—and that he wanted to deepen his poetry skills. By the time we said goodnight, we were fast friends.

I was about to offer an online course through a website called 24 Pearl Street, called "Working the Beat: How to Make Poems Sing," from November 7 to 11, and Jeffrey told me he might want to sign up. To my delight, he did. He was an absolute joy in the online workshop, full of humor and enthusiasm. Not surprisingly a natural leader, he was open and generous with the other poets, sharing his struggles and triumphs in this new world of meter in a way that put everyone at ease.

I am used to my meter classes blowing people's minds; to learn how to create poetic effects you've never dreamed possible is a powerful thrill. But no matter how many times I've seen it happen, sometimes it just takes my breath away to share in the experience of a poet who is especially open and ready to appreciate and absorb the potentially earth-shaking impact of this teaching. It was amazing to see how readily and deeply the power of meter transformed Jeffrey's poetic voice.

Even though Jeffrey Betcher had arrived at the class with zero metrical knowledge, he waded fearlessly, head-on, into the succession of rhythmic waves, engaging each new meter with dedication and gusto, allowing the wave to gather its full strength, breathing steadily, staying calm, remembering his focus, not stopping until he had a serious poem. By the end of the four-week class, he was competent to write and scan trochees, iambs, dactyls, and anapests.

Jeffrey was so excited to be working on his poetry again that he sent me his poetry chapbook manuscript "The Fucking Seasons" for my feedback on November 10 and began weekly private poetry consultations with me just after "Working the Beat" ended. On November 21 he wrote me an email with the subject header, "I'm having such fun," including a light verse poem about a visit to his doctor. I also helped him edit lyrics for a sweet gay love song called "Love Me Main Street." By November 28 we were working hard on editing "The Fucking Seasons" into a publishable volume, and soon after he began submitting it to contests.

Somewhere along the line, Jeffrey opened one of our phone conferences by telling me he had been diagnosed with terminal cancer. This knowledge radically changed the nature of our work together. Within seconds of him sharing the news we entered into an unspoken agreement to switch frequencies, into a space that was at once deeper and more serious and lighter, sweeter, more daringly true. It was as if the kinship we had felt since our first meeting was now given full permission to bloom.

With the chapbook editing finished and this earth-shattering change of perspective, Jeffrey was eager to start on a new project. He wanted to write about his experience with the diagnosis, the medical regimens he was facing, and his evolving feelings about mortality. When he asked my advice about what form I thought would work well for what both of us felt would be his last poetic undertaking, I suggested a crown of sonnets. This is a form consisting of fourteen sonnets, each beginning with the last line of the previous sonnet, plus a final sonnet that is created from the final lines of all the others. It is an ambitious, monumental poetic form that allows space for multiple perspectives, moods, and experiences within a single larger framework. Jeffrey liked the idea, and based on his experience in the meter class, we agreed on the capacious, lively anapestic meter as the best one for the project.

Jeffrey dove into his anapestic sonnet crown with his characteristic gusto, professionalism, and high standards. I knew by now that he was that kind of a person. And I certainly knew first-hand how remarkably well he had developed his metrical knowledge in my "Working the Beat" class—yet still, given that he had never written poems in meter until one month before, his first sonnet took my breath away. This was not a typical beginner's sonnet. It sang, it delved, it flew. I felt I was witnessing one of those amazing moments—like Rilke's *Duono Elegies* or Sylvia Plath's *Ariel* poems—where a poet, a form, a voice, and a subject come together into a dance that feels predestined for immortality.

Each week Jeffrey would bring a new sonnet to our phone conference and we would go over it, syllable by syllable, stress by stress, anapest by anapest, line by line. And each week the sonnet would stand up to the scrutiny. Often, in fact— as I have found to be the case with the greatest poems— the most technical discussions opened doorways into the most philosophical and spiritual levels and aspects of the poem. Take our discussion of these lines from Sonnet 10, for example:

> When we die, it's distraction, a gnat of a knell,
> Where malignancy, heart beat, and ghost become
> friends,

Jeffrey was concerned that a variation he had made in the third foot of the second line quoted might be a problem, so he asked what I thought. Quick detour for a definition: a "foot" is a repeating rhythmic unit. The anapestic foot that Jeffrey had chosen as the basis for this crown of sonnets has three syllables, with the first two pronounced softly and the third stressed more loudly. If you read (*aloud*, please!!) any of the sonnets in this book, you will hear that Jeffrey tended to honor this anapestic rhythm quite closely. But there are variations, too—times when the rhythm changes to shift tone or emphasis. We were discussing one of those variation moments.

The third foot of the second line, "beat and ghost," scans with a loud first syllable instead of the expected soft syllable (using scansion marks, we would mark the foot as / **u** / instead of the expected anapestic pattern of **u u** /). My approach to questions like this one is always to read the passage aloud several times, meditating deeply on the meaning of the lines in connection with the rhythm, weighing whether the change adds to a reader's understanding of the line's depths and experience of its impact. As Jeffrey and I weighed the meaning of this third foot together, it became clear that the loud "beat" of the heart in that metrically unexpected place was the perfect way to convey the growing importance of his awareness of the amazing fact of living.

At another point in the sonnet crown, Jeffrey wanted to talk about the line in Sonnet 4, "It seems Death pulls on pants one gaunt leg at a time." We laughed deliciously about that line, how the meter forces you to slow down and stress each syllable of "one gaunt leg," making the image even funnier, slowing it down to the speed and tempo of pulling on those pants. Preparing this preface, I came across a note I had written: "laughed with Jeffrey about how 'gaunt leg' is earned, because "humor is important" …."That was one of the beautiful lessons I learned from my hours spent with Jeffrey during the year before his death: that humor is important.

By June, Jeffrey had a full draft of the sonnet sequence, at that time called "Gravity Waits." We continued to work on it over the summer, as he moved closer and closer to death. He sent me a draft of the crown with the new title, "Whistling Through," on September 29. On October 14 I wrote to him,

> Dearest Jeffrey,
>
> Finally have my computer back and working, and I'm ready to put in those small edits with Track Changes.
>
> But I can't do it on the PDF version.
>
> Will you please send this again in Word doc format, and I will turn it around right away? I'm also wondering whether you wanted to do anything about the three slightly bigger edits that I flagged in my text to you, before we send it out for publication.
>
> I'm eager to talk again. Let me know when is good.
>
> Hugs,
> Annie

We spoke on the phone a few days later. Though his voice was weak, he sounded happy and satisfied as he told me he liked the changes I had suggested. I told him that in my estimation, with those changes the sonnet crown was now finished. It seemed perfect. I had no more suggestions. And he felt the same way. We shared a beautiful moment together as I congratulated him on what I was sure then, as I am sure now, is a major poem, an important contribution to anapestic poetry in English, to gay literature, to the form of the crown of sonnets, and to the literature of mortality.

Jeffrey Betcher passed over on October 21, 2017. I expect that he would like nothing better than to know that this book is being published in time for what would have been his 62nd birthday. I hope that *Whistling Through,* his final gift to the world, will live on for a long, long time. I am honored to publish it for the first time in this chapbook from Poetry Witch Press.

Annie Finch
Brooklyn, New York
June 6, 2022

PS When I told Jeffrey that some amazing experiences had convinced me of death's beauty, he was eager to hear about them. On May 16, 2017 we recorded one of our phone conversations on this topic, followed by a conversation about edits to the crown of sonnets. The audio of this conversation is now posted online at the Poetry Witch Press website.

Whistling Through

By
Jeffrey Betcher

1. Diagnosis

Diagnosis is terminal. Life finds its shape
A few feet from the ground as it tries to take flight
In a fog of dead air, with a load of dead weight,
And a pilot who's just lost all feeling and sight.
I can hear the unknowable next whistling through ...
... Through bright holes in a scan, through my fingers and bones,
Through the cracks in my plans ... whistling right through.
It's the sound of a song I must sing, but don't know.
Life can syncopate: music, familiar but strange,
As the rhythm of spirit and flesh swells and fades,
Innuendo from angels that gravity waits
For this tangle of melody ... death ... to unbraid.
In the time it takes sunrise to free the day's light,
"It's not good news," can sum up the faint sounds of night.

2. Wall

"It's not good news" can sum up the faint sounds of night.
I can hear, over doctors and daylight, the noise
Of a half-life in pieces that's starting to rise
As through mud, like the pit from when I was a boy.
Dark release (now I know my death's "how," if not "when")
Seems to bubble up first, a blah-BLOOP in the room.
Then the ruckus of leaving my friends rocks my head
With a quiet as loud as when water breaks womb.
And then Wham! there's a wall, existential cement,
Staggered stones cut with questions and mortared with fate.
Life's no more than it seems, then we die, and then ... next?
If an answer exists, it comes one breath too late.
Prickly devils play tag on my neck's oily nape,
Between symptom and grave, as my life hangs agape.

3. Mind-Fuck

Between symptom and grave, as my life hangs agape,
Waits ba-RUM-bump, both wry and awry with it all.
So I cackle from fear … out of turn, short of rage …
As Absurdity's mind-fuck pins faith to the wall.
Ask philosopher, clergy, clinician alike:
Is it random, this cancer? Genetic? Bad luck?
Psychological sin or Pat Robertson tripe,
Like the backhand of God or creative self-fuck?
What a buttload of judgement I'm fighting today.
Anal tumors … together as big as a cock …
Up a gay guy? PuhLEASE! I don't fuck me that way.
And yet scrupulous ass answers tumorous knock.
It seems Death pulls on pants one gaunt leg at a time,
As my body is tricked, by itself, of its life.

4. Treatment

As my body is tricked, by itself, of its life
I tell all who might care that I'm day facing night,
And renege on all plans but incurable strife.
Jarring news, like my cancer, proves far from benign
In the body of family, system of friends.
My community, wobbling from things that I've said,
Still forestalls my ascension (ethereal bends),
And makes sure mid-anew is well-sung and well-fed.
I'm ceviche to half-deadly chemical brines.
I've been patient with doctors still learning their craft.
I've absorbed radiation, been under the knife,
Altared crystal and cross with medicinal laughs.
Alas, butt-rot's not gurgling and draining away,
Why not strip mine some bliss from a cancerous day?

5. La-Z-Boy

Why not strip mine some bliss from a cancerous day,
Like reclining with iPad and pot and TV?
My front room, where a La-Z-Boy's muscled its way,
Holds adjustable, wireless, and stoned death for me.
I've decided that life must end here or in bed,
Much like Dad slumping cancerous lungs near TV.
(My recliner recalls this, and fucks with my head.
I smell 'boros, Ensure … there's a faint scent of pee.)
Or like Mom, who withstood an ovarian bomb,
Then chose nursing facility over her home:
Country mile of relief between self-care and calm,
Magic call-button, sheet changes, time left alone.
As I cradle these crags from the tree of my bloom,
My Gethsemane grows in a windowless room.

6. Wishbone

My Gethsemane grows in a windowless room
In a Mission Bay building at UCSF,
Through door A, off a lobby of guesses and gloom
Where the sick hug their shadows. I pray for the best.
"It's annoying as hell," my onc, Chloe, confides
As my gut, doing somersaults, loops on a screen.
A CT scan shows cancer's spread up from behind
To my liver. Malignity turning obscene.
If prognosis and miracle pull on my arms,
(I'm a wishbone divining if cancer will roam
To my death or anomaly: truncated harm)
I see faith, and not stats, holding nub of snapped bone.
But, as need outgrows time at the end of our day,
Resignation and faith start to share DNA.

7. Returns

Resignation and faith start to share DNA
As I probe life's resiliency, looking for leaks.
Expectation and instinct corrode, fail and flake
Into carpets of rust dust beneath spirit feet.
I can breath from two airs. I can drink from two worlds.
I feel angels insinuate, escorts implore.
My heart pounds this sheer shore and faint blood tendrils swirl.
Did I turn off the iron and do all my chores?
I return. Just like that. All I knew did await.
Beneath drowsiness beats the ole fidget and yearn,
Cooling dreams leave me feeling a lover's embrace,
And return to mundanity eases concern.
Still, the wavelength of cancer spans heaven and doom.
When we step from ourselves, our bravado breathes fumes.

8. Leaving

When we step from ourselves, our bravado breathes fumes,
And divines how it's reasons for living have changed.
Is there something to learn from the dying, the fugues
Of the wasted, the weakened, the remnant, the aged?
Come and sit in a place that is fearfully still,
Where a faraway gaze can slice burden from bone,
Where the day simply won't, but the night surely will,
Where the gases collect, and eruptions atone.
I don't know what will be after making my way
From the place that we are, from the time that we've shared.
Will it help you to be here the day I can't stay?
All I know is there's love left in bodies stripped bare.
Even here, done with mending, while Death apprehends,
Even now, I believe, it's not really the end.

9. Interruptions

Even now, I believe, it's not really the end,
Just a certain predictable shift, interrup-
Tion, a winter, snowed-in, when it's fine to pretend
Time is punctual, calendars never ice up.
Some slick season is this, as my ego, hosed down
With disease and toxicity, slips. And my mind
Clicks cold fobs, in the seams of its pockets. Re-found:
Random peach pit and petal dust, corkage from wine.
Folks succeed all the time. It's not difficult. Death.
Just exquisite refraction of aging, misfortune, and ills.
Life beyond our round world is rock-steady of breath.
It expands as we spin, as it has, as we will.
Ask of Death, "Should I yield?" It is Life that foretells
When we die, it's distraction, a gnat of a knell.

10. Gnats

When we die, it's distraction, a gnat of a knell.
Even wounds, deep and mortal, forget how to bleed.
Dying shifts, takes the shape of our fears and farewells,
As we learn: death's invasive and common as weeds.
Just as children will grow without knowledge of why,
Just as life leads to love when we aren't in the way,
So our bodies assure us they know how to die,
To relieve us of pain with the tools of decay.
In a world swelled with guns, anger, arrogance, greed,
In which people build fences, dig shelters, draw blinds,
I am lucky my killer is cellular-me,
And my loved ones, with love, can my leaving align.
Absence IS; it's substantial, and slow to unbend
Where malignancy, heart beat, and ghost become friends.

11. Instinct

Where malignancy, heart beat, and ghost become friends
Is a lawless, unruly last moment and place.
I'm to finally pass through aversion to ends?
Through infinitive split between instinct and grace?
I believe this world comes with a natural law,
Often served from the breast over giggles and cries,
One that rules us as surely as biscuits rule dogs.
Whereas: life is where touch lives, so we must survive.
I am not dead, today, but today is not done.
The inscrutable cat in me calculates paths
From the deck, where I'm warm from the afternoon sun,
To a bramble of shadows and mice from the past.
Disobedient life joins unruly farewell.
It's why angels respond. It's a practical spell.

12. Dancing

It's why angels respond. It's a practical spell
On an acre of love you can't see from the road.
So suspiciously leafy ... there must be a well.
Gentle scent. Scented song. Curiosity's glow.
I envision a fence, on a lick of high land,
That bemuses the sky and bedazzles the ground.
It's a distant relation who touches my hand,
And says, "Cancer and fence are about to come down."
I am sowing my step a foot deep in the dance.
Atmospherical lungs sway my grave, heal my ass,
Billow life into dust, and lull dust into trance
As I dance to the rhythm of breath through tall grass.
Without cause, without consequence, trillions of cells
Come apart and join hands as while the universe swells.

13. Drowsing

Come apart and join hands whileas the universe swells.
Loyal body: sit up, welcome ghosts gathered near.
Deathbed dream: nudge the wild, and all distance dispel.
Loves I'm leaving: take comfort, love can't disappear.
As we grow toward our lives, light is sung, sounds are seen.
Emanating love's rhythm is god, goal and gift.
Life's not yours. It's not mine. It's the music between ...
... Between us, between worlds ... where reality drifts.
Now I'm swept by a choir to the center-most pew
Where, in mingling of voice, birth and death become clear.
At my feet, dust is moved and a spirit accrues
As the walls and the rafters, with song, drench my ears.
Now I linger and listen to ringers and bells.
I'm awake, dreaming life, despite drugs and rogue cells.

14. Seconal

I'm awake, dreaming life, despite drugs and rogue cells
That make room for infection that fracks my behind.
I'm awake after surgeons have cut what rebels.
I'm afloat in the lining of my peace of mind.
I have hithered and yonned a holistic blue sky,
And refracted myself through an evidence base.
So, please trust when I rate Marijuana quite high
On thea scale: lazy leaches to practical grace.
Same with cocktails that twist up my dying with fun.
True. Champagne and a Zofran quelled chemo the most,
So I thought, why not drink through this cancer with 1)
Sloshy sanctity, 2) middle finger, or both.
Massive privilege, this, putting death on my terms.
With physician assistance, I'll turn my own worm.

15. Weightlessness

Diagnosis is terminal. Life finds its shape.
"It's not good news" can sum up the faint sounds of night,
Between symptom and grave, as my life hangs agape,
As my body is tricked, by itself, of its life.
Why not strip mine some bliss from a cancerous day?
My Gethsemane grows in a windowless room.
Resignation and faith start to share DNA.
When we step from ourselves, our bravado breathes fumes.
Even now, I believe, it's not really the end.
When we die, it's distraction, a gnat of a knell,
Where malignancy, heart beat, and ghost become friends.
It's why angels respond. It's a practical spell.
Come apart and join hands as the universe swells.
I'm awake, dreaming life, despite drugs and rogue cells.

Reminiscences

Visiting Jeffrey Betcher was a treat even before we got to his house. My late wife Patricia

Monaghan and I visited Jeffrey twice, and I visited him alone once after her death. Arriving at his address on Quesada, our attention was drawn by a lush, developed garden in the median strip of the road. It seemed like Jeffrey's nurturing heart had transcended the walls of his house and spread out into the street, touching everyone who passed by.

Entering the house we experienced a sense of hospitality and welcomeness that was remarkable. We felt we had known him forever. He had sought us out because his work and Patricia's overlapped. In our visits we all shared talk about serious and humorous events in our recent lives. We felt comfort and intimacy in his presence.

After Patricia died, Jeffrey made sure I visited again. And, again, I felt a sense of belonging. It was during this visit that I learned more about the Quesada Garden Initiative, and Jeffrey's role. The median had been a locale of garbage and even crime. Jeffrey, along with other community members, decided to fill the once trash-filled strip with vegetable and flower plots. Despite struggles with the city, Jeffrey and the others persevered and Quesada Gardens remains flourishing, living on as a memory of Jeffrey's smile and love.

—*Michael McDermott*

Sometimes when you lose a close friend, it's like there's a tear in space where they once were. Such was the case with Jeffrey Betcher who left us in 2017, and for me and his close circle of friends, we never really got over it. Jeffrey was a friend for all seasons, who could slide from a dive bar to a black tie event with aplomb, and was always there for you. These last years have been such a shit show, made even more so without Jeffrey's opinions, camaraderie, and counsel. WWJS indeed!

Facing a terminal diagnosis, Jeffrey passed the torch of his community activism to his colleagues, and he returned to perhaps his core identity— the soul of a poet. And while he worked on revisiting and revising earlier poems, he also took on the herculean task of confronting his impending death, the indignities of cancer, and the meaning of leaving, all while banging on the door of the Great Beyond. This was his epic poem "Whistling Through."

Why did he choose the thorny form of a crown of sonnets for his final expression? Perhaps, it was a way to exert control in words over a physical situation he could not alter. No matter— the result is an alchemical transmutation where his ordeal becomes a no-holds-barred odyssey that's profound, funny, terrifying, and utterly dazzling.

—*Lex Nover*
February 2022

Left "believing in the pack mentality of strays," the poetry of Jeffrey Betcher speaks from the entire collective of American queer stray culture, that very lost-and-found narrative of reinvention on the docks of survival. These docks, being the green-heeled sanctuary of San Francisco from 1986-2016, these docks gave birth to an examination and liberation of meaning, as wildly honest and true-to-mirror as every queer breath we've danced. From Jeffrey Betcher's poetry collection "The Fucking Seasons, Selected Poems 1986 to 2016," we hear the journeys into witness, touch the lips of knowing "love has been here. Hungry footsteps, breath released, and touch can change the land forever." His intimate poetry was cultivated over the decades, exploring survival and engagement, and the labyrinth of the heart. Though he dodged the HIV bullet in the plague-torn years, a terminal bout of cancer cut his life short in 2017. In addition to his chapbook of Selected Poems (1986-2016), he completed an epic sonnet, *Whistling Through*, an odyssey into the cancer machine and death itself.

—*Toussaint St. Negritude*

CPSIA information can be obtained
at www.ICGtesting.com
Printed in the USA
LVHW081303270423
745479LV00007B/154